PARIS UNVEILED

A Comprehensive Travel Guide to the City of Love 2023

Curtis J. O'Neill

Copyright © 2023 by Curtis J. O'Neill All rights reserved. No part of this publication may be reproduced, distributed, or transmitted in any form or by any means, including photocopying, recording, or other electronic or mechanical methods, without the prior written permission of the publisher, except in the case of brief quotations embodied in critical reviews and certain other noncommercial uses permitted by copyright law.

TABLE OF CONTENTS

CHAPTER 1 7

BONJOUR, PARIS! 7

    Paris History and Culture 7

    Understanding Parisian Etiquette 12

    Best Times to Visit Paris 16

    Parisian Transportation Basics 19

CHAPTER 2 23

FROM THE EIFFEL TOWER TO THE LOUVRE
.... 23

    The Eiffel Tower: History and Facts 23

    The Champs-Élysées and Arc de Triomphe 26

    The Louvre Museum: Must-See Artworks and Exhibits 30

    Notre-Dame Cathedral and Sainte-Chapelle 33

CHAPTER 3 36

NAVIGATING THE ARRONDISSEMENTS 36

    The Latin Quarter: History and Highlights 36

The Marais: Trendy Neighborhood and Attractions 39

Montmartre: The Bohemian District of Paris ... 42

The Seine River: Cruising and Walking Tours . 45

CHAPTER 4 48

CUISINE CAPITAL 48

French Food: A Brief History 48

Classic French Dishes to Try in Paris 51

Bistros, Brasseries, and Michelin-Starred Restaurants 54

Food Markets and Specialty Shops 56

CHAPTER 5 59

HIDDEN GEMS AND LOCAL HANGOUTS 59

Canal Saint-Martin: A Quirky Neighborhood with Hidden Gems 59

Parc des Buttes-Chaumont: A Serene Green Space in the City 65

Promenade Plantée: Paris's Secret Garden Walkway 68

Village Saint-Paul: A Labyrinth of Antique Shops and Art Galleries 71

CHAPTER 6 75

ROMANCE IN PARIS 75

Romantic Walks: Strolls Along the Seine and Beyond 75

Classic Parisian Experiences for Couples 78

Best Romantic Restaurants and Bars 81

Exploring Paris's Romantic Past and Present ... 84

CHAPTER 7 87

ART AND CULTURE 87

Paris Museums and Art Galleries 87

Art Nouveau and Art Deco Architecture in Paris 90

Famous French Artists and Their Works 93

Performing Arts and Festivals in Paris 96

CHAPTER 8 99

SHOPPING AND FASHION 99

Parisian Fashion: A Brief History 99

    Fashion Boutiques and Department Stores 102

    Vintage and Second-Hand Shopping in Paris . 106

    Parisian Fashion and Style Tips 109

CHAPTER 9 111

OUTDOOR ADVENTURES 111

    Parks and Gardens in Paris 111

    Biking and Hiking Trails in and Around the City
    114

    Day Trips to Natural Wonders Near Paris 119

CHAPTER 10 122

BEYOND THE CITY LIMITS 122

    Palace of Versailles: A Day Trip to the Lavish
    Royal Residence 122

    Champagne Tasting in Reims and Épernay 125

    Normandy D-Day Beaches: A Historic and
    Scenic Tour 128

    The Loire Valley: Castles, Wine, and More ... 132

CHAPTER 1

BONJOUR, PARIS!

Paris History and Culture

France's main city, Paris, has a long and storied past and culture. Paris has had a major impact on European history and society from the time of the Roman invasion to the present. This chapter offers a broad summary of Paris's history and culture by examining significant figures, occasions, and locations that have influenced the city.

Paris History

The Gauls, a Celtic people who were subjugated by the Romans in the first century BC, are the first documented residents of the Paris area. On the location of modern-day Paris, the Romans founded a village named Lutetia, which developed over the following several centuries into a thriving metropolis.

Paris developed into a hub for learning, culture, and the arts during the Middle Ages, serving as the capitol of the Kingdom of France.

During this period, Gothic building thrived, as evidenced by the famous Notre-Dame Cathedral and Sainte-Chapelle. In the 17th and 18th centuries, Paris developed into a center for Enlightenment theory and thought, with contributors to the period's intellectual dialogue including Voltaire, Rousseau, and Diderot.

Paris's past was altered by the French Revolution of 1789. A revolt by the people that resulted in the fall of the monarchy and the founding of the First French Republic was ignited by the assault of the Bastille jail, an emblem of regal oppression. The French people battled for liberty, equity, and brotherhood during the Revolution, which was a period of significant political turmoil and societal change.

Under the direction of Emperor Napoleon III, Paris underwent a significant urban transformation in the 19th century, becoming the modern, expansive city it is today.

Haussmann's renovations, which included the construction of broad boulevards, public parks, and grand buildings, transformed Paris into the city we know today.

Paris was significantly impacted by both of the World Wars that characterized the 20th century. major conflicts took place in Paris during World War I, which resulted in major harm to or destruction of the city's iconic monuments. Due to Nazi troops' prolonged occupation of Paris during World War II, the destruction was even worse. However, as a hub for art, fashion, and academic life following the war, Paris underwent a cultural and commercial revival.

French Culture

With a thriving arts community that includes everything from theater and ballet to writing and music, Paris has long been regarded as a cultural hub. The city is home to many galleries and art places in addition to some of the most well-known institutions in the world, such as the Louvre, the Musée d'Orsay, and the Centre Pompidou.

With a wide variety of gastronomic customs that represent the city's ethnic past, Paris is also well known for its food.

A staple of Parisian eating is French food, which places a focus on fresh products and refined display. However, the city also provides a wide variety of other cuisines, including Middle Eastern, Asian, Italian, and Spanish.

Paris is renowned for its design and style in addition to its cultural attractions. The city is a center for cutting-edge fashion and design and is home to some of the most well-known fashion companies in the world, such as Chanel, Dior, and Yves Saint Laurent.

Last but not least, Paris is a metropolis with a rich heritage of writing, philosophy, and thought. It has a great profundity of cerebral and psychological thought. Some of the most significant authors and philosophers in history have drawn ingenuity and inspiration from Paris, from the philosophical works of Jean-Paul Sartre and Simone de Beauvoir to the poems of Charles Baudelaire and Paul Verlaine.

Paris' character and allure are fundamentally shaped by its past and culture.

The city has a thriving and varied cultural legacy that includes philosophy, design, writing, and the arts. Significant occurrences throughout its history, such as the Roman invasion and the French Revolution, have molded the city's identity and added to its lasting impact. Paris's past and culture must be fully appreciated in order to fully enjoy the city's many draws.

By visiting its museums, galleries, historic sites, and lively districts, as well as by delighting in its food, fashion, and cerebral life, visitors to Paris can submerge themselves in its history and culture. Paris continues to be one of the most intriguing and alluring places in the world. Here, the past and present cohabit in a vibrant and enthralling equilibrium.

Understanding Parisian Etiquette

Millions of tourists from all over the world travel to Paris, the City of Light, each year because it is a major artistic and social center. As a result, in order to fully enjoy the city, one must be familiar with Parisian manners. An unspoken code of conduct that governs everything from pleasantries and clothing standards to eating and conversation is known as Parisian protocol. This chapter gives a general summary of Parisian decorum and examines some of the most important traditions and manners that travelers to Paris should be aware of.

Salutation and Interaction

Communication and welcome are two of Parisian etiquette's most crucial facets. Depending on the degree of intimacy, it is traditional to welcome individuals in Paris with a greeting or a peck on the face. It is acceptable to use polite names, like "Monsieur" or "Madame," when meeting someone for the first time until they encourage you to use their first name.

Parisians respect honesty and directness in conversation, but they also demand a certain amount of decency and tact. It's crucial to refrain from interjecting when people are talking and to pay close attention to what they have to say. In general, Parisians are not hesitant to voice their views and may get into heated arguments, but they also value deference and polite conversation.

Fashion Code

Paris is known as the center of fashion, and people there take pride in their looks. As a result, it's crucial to wear suitable clothing when in the metropolis. When attending eateries, museums, and other cultural places, it is advised to dress more officially even though informal clothing is appropriate in some situations, such as parks and cafés.

In general, Parisians dress elegantly and subtly, putting an emphasis on premium fabrics and timeless silhouettes.

Additionally, it's crucial to refrain from donning garish or noisy apparel as this might be interpreted as improper or attention-seeking.

Dining Manners

Dining out is a crucial component of Parisian society because the city is known for its food. As a result, in order to fully enjoy the city's gastronomic offerings, one must be aware of proper eating manners.

Depending on the degree of acquaintance, it's traditional to give your fellow guests a greeting or a peck on the face when you meet them at the table in Paris. Additionally, it's crucial to wait until everyone has been served before starting to consume and to refrain from conversing or otherwise creating sounds while doing so.

Prior to the main dish, it is traditional to order a drink and an entrée, and following the dinner, it is conventional to order cake and coffee or tea. Respecting Paris's wine culture, where wine is frequently matched with cuisine and consumed in restraint, is also essential.

In summation, anyone hoping to fully experience the city of Paris must be familiar with Parisian decorum. An unspoken code of conduct that governs everything from pleasantries and clothing standards to eating and conversation is known as Parisian protocol. Visitors can honor Parisian culture and develop close relationships with its citizens by adhering to these traditions and manners. Finally, in order to completely immerse oneself in the city's vibrant and varied social and cultural life, one must grasp Parisian decorum.

Best Times to Visit Paris

All year long, Paris is a stunning and energetic metropolis. But there are some seasons of the year when going to the metropolis can be especially pleasant and unforgettable. We will discuss the ideal times to visit Paris in this chapter based on variables like the temperature, people, and activities.

Spring (March to May)

Paris is a fantastic place to explore in the spring. With temps ranging between 11°C and 18°C (52°F and 64°F), the climate is pleasant, and the city's renowned gardens and parks are in full blossom. The city's major sites are simpler to traverse because there are fewer people present than during the busiest summer months. The Paris Marathon, the French Open Tennis Tournament, and the June Festival of Music are additional attractions for visitors.

Summer (June to August)

Millions of tourists swarm to Paris during the summer to take advantage of the mild temperatures, lengthy days, and outdoor events. The weather is generally mild, with average highs of 20°C to 25°C (68°F to 77°F), but it can also get very steamy and muggy. Open-air performances, cinema events, and the celebrated Bastille Day pyrotechnics on July 14th are all available to visitors. However, the throngs can be oppressive and there may be lengthy lines at well-known sites like the Louvre and the Eiffel Tower.

Fall (September to November)

Paris is also fantastic in the fall. The throngs are fewer, temps range from 8°C to 18°C (46°F to 64°F), and the fall greenery gives the city's parks and gardens a special appeal. Visitors can take part in activities like the Autumn Festival, the International Contemporary Art Fair, and Paris Fashion Week.

Winter (December to February)

Paris during the winter can be particularly enchanting, especially around the holidays. Visitors can enjoy ice skating, Christmas markets, and the renowned New Year's Eve pyrotechnics at the Champs-Élysées while the city is dressed out in holiday lights. Although the city is comparatively less congested and has chilly weather with average temps ranging from 3°C to 8°C (37°F to 46°F), tourists can still enjoy the city's interior sights like museums, galleries, and shows.

Paris is a fantastic place to explore all year round, but the ideal time to go relies on personal tastes and interests. While summer and winter offer distinctive celebrations and activities but can be congested and weather-dependent, spring and autumn offer pleasant weather, fewer crowds, and a diversity of cultural events. In the end, travelers to Paris are guaranteed to have an unforgettable experience no matter what time of year they come because of the city's grandeur, charisma, and cultural diversity.

Parisian Transportation Basics

The superb transit system in Paris makes getting around the city very simple for tourists. The fundamentals of Parisian transportation, such as the different forms of transportation accessible, ticket choices, and advice for traversing the city, will be covered in this chapter.

Transportation Methods

There are numerous ways to get around Paris, including:

Paris Metro: Getting around the city is easiest and quickest using the Paris Metro. It has 300 stops, 16 routes, and a total distance of more than 200 km (125 mi). The everyday train schedule is 5:30 am to 1:15 am, with more frequent service during the morning rush.

transportation: Paris has a robust and all-encompassing transportation infrastructure. It is a great choice for tourists who want to walk around the city and take in the sights.

From 5:30 am to late, buses operate on various lines, including some that run at night.

RER: The RER is a network of regional fast trains that links Paris with its outlying areas. For traveling outside of the city core, it is a quicker choice.

Taxis: Although commonplace in Paris, taxi fares can be high. They work best for brief journeys or at nighttime transport.

Ticket Choices

A variety of tickets are available for use on Paris's public transit system. These consist of:

Single Tickets: Within Paris, a single ticket is good for just one ride on the RER, bus, or metro. It is good for one hour and thirty minutes and costs €1.90.

Packs of passes: A "carnet," which is a pack of ten passes, costs €16.90.

Day Passes: A day ticket, known as a "Mobilis," entitles the holder to one day of unrestricted use of Paris's RER, transport, and Metro systems. A zone 1-2 ticket costs €7.50 as a starting point.

The Navigo ticket is a weekly or monthly ticket that entitles the holder to unrestricted use of the Metro, transport, and RER in Paris and its surrounding areas. The price of the weekly ticket is €22.80, while the monthly pass is €75.20.

Advice for Getting Around Paris

For newcomers, navigating Paris can be daunting. The following advice will help you journey more comfortably:

Use a plan or a navigation tool on your phone to avoid getting disoriented in Paris' maze of streets and alleyways. You can move around the city more quickly by using a guide or a smartphone software like Google Maps.

Travel outside of rush hours: In Paris, rush hours are from 7 am to 9 am and from 5 pm to 7 pm. If at all feasible, try to stay away from these hours to escape packed railroads and vehicles.

Paris is renowned for its pickpocketing, so be on the lookout for them. Secure your belongings, and pay attention to your surroundings.

Use the same ticket for transfers: If you're changing means of transit, like from the Metro to the bus, you can use the same ticket.

The city of Paris has an excellent transit system that makes getting around the city simple. Compared to getting a cab, using the Metro, transport, and RER can save you time and money. You can traverse the city like an expert and take in all of Paris' sights and noises with a little advance planning and preparation.

CHAPTER 2

FROM THE EIFFEL TOWER TO THE LOUVRE

The Eiffel Tower: History and Facts

One of the most popular tourism destinations in the world and a recognizable representation of Paris is the Eiffel Tower. We will look at the details and background of the Eiffel Tower in this part.

History

For the Paris World's Fair in 1889, which commemorated the 100th anniversary of the French Revolution, the Eiffel Tower was constructed. Gustave Eiffel, a French architect who also created the structure for the Statue of Liberty in New York, was responsible for its construction.

More than 18,000 sections of cast iron and 2.5 million bolts were used during the tower's construction, which started in 1887 and was finished in just two years.

The skyscraper, which stood at 324 meters and was formally unveiled on March 31, 1889, was the highest man-made building in the globe at the time. (1,063 feet).

The skyscraper was originally only supposed to last for 20 years, but it was spared from being demolished and is now a constant feature of the Paris cityscape. Millions of people tour it every year and it is still one of the most recognized sites in the globe today.

Facts

Over 10,000 tons of cast iron make up the 18,038 parts that make up the Eiffel Tower.

Visitors can access three floors of the structure. While the third floor can only be reached by lift, the first and second levels can both be accessed via steps.

Each night, the tower's 20,000 light lights are illuminated.

Originally coated in 25 different hues of brown, the structure is now given a fresh coat of paint every seven years that requires about 60 kilograms of paint.

In the early 20th century, the tower was used for radio communication; it is still in use today for television and radio programming.

When there are heavy gusts, the structure can shift up to 7 centimeters (2.75 inches) in motion.

The daughter of Gustave Eiffel, Thomas Edison, and even Hitler during the Nazi siege of Paris are just a few of the notable people who have visited the tower over the years.

The Eiffel Tower is evidence of the French people's inventiveness and originality. One of the most popular and recognizable sites in the world, it has endured the weight of time. The history and details of the tower offer an intriguing look into the creation and development of this famous building. Any visitor to Paris must see the Eiffel Tower, which is guaranteed to make an enduring impact.

The Champs-Élysées and Arc de Triomphe

Two of Paris' most well-known monuments, the Champs-Élysées and the Arc de Triomphe, draw millions of tourists each year. We will examine the background and importance of these recognizable landmarks in this chapter.

Les Champs-Élysées

A well-known thoroughfare in Paris, the Champs-Élysées, connects the Arc de Triomphe to the Place de la Concorde. One of the most prominent locations in Paris, it is surrounded with stores, eateries, and cafés. Many of the city's artistic icons, including the Grand Palais and the Petit Palais, are located on the road.

In the 17th century, the Champs-Élysées was initially built as an opulent entryway to the Tuileries Palace. After being subsequently expanded to its present extent in the 19th century, it rose to popularity among both Parisians and tourists.

The road is now known for its fashion shows, marches, and cultural events and serves as a representation of Parisian grandeur.

The Triumphal Arch

At the western extremity of the Champs-Élysées is a ceremonial structure known as the Arc de Triomphe. Napoleon Bonaparte ordered it in 1806 to honor his triumphs and the valor of his troops. The bridge is 50 meters (164 feet) tall and was finished in 1836.

Napoleon's wars and the French Revolution are two significant events in French history that are represented in statues and reliefs that decorate the bridge. Under the gateway, the Unknown Soldier's Tomb is located, and a light is lit in his honor.

Atop the Arc de Triomphe, visitors can get a bird's-eye perspective of the metropolis. At night, when the city is illuminated, the view from the summit is particularly stunning.

Two of Paris' most recognizable monuments, the Champs-Élysées and the Arc de Triomphe, are immersed in importance and history. Anyone who wishes to experience the refinement and glitz of Parisian living must visit the Champs-Élysées, while the Arc de Triomphe provides a look into France's illustrious military past. These two sites provide tourists with a diverse cultural experience and are a must-see on any trip to Paris.

The Louvre Museum: Must-See Artworks and Exhibits

With millions of tourists each year, the Louvre Museum ranks among the most popular tourist destinations in the globe. The Louvre is a must-visit location for any art enthusiast with its extensive collection of works of art and relics covering thousands of years. We'll look at a few of the Louvre Museum's must-see artworks and displays in this part.

Mona Lisa

Perhaps the most well-known piece of art in the Louvre Museum is the Mona Lisa, which was created by Leonardo da Vinci. The artwork shows a lady with a cryptic grin, and because of its ambiguous nature, it has become one of the most recognizable pictures in history. Visitors to the Louvre can get a close-up look at the artwork and admire its deft brushstrokes and nuanced coloring.

Victory of Milo

Aphrodite is depicted in the old Greek monument known as the Venus de Milo. The figure was found in 1820 on the island of Milos, and the Louvre purchased it in 1821. One of the most significant pieces of ancient Greek art, the Venus de Milo is renowned for its lovely contours and sensitive features.

Victory of Samothrace with Wings

Nike, the Greek deity of triumph, is depicted in the Winged triumph of Samothrace. On the island of Samothrace, the monument was found in 1863, and the Louvre bought it in 1884. Nike appears to be going forward as though captured in a triumphant moment in the Winged Victory, which is renowned for its dramatic composition.

Apartments for Napoleon III

The French ruler Napoleon III and his wife Eugénie once resided in a group of luxurious chambers known as the Napoleon III Apartments.

The lavishly adorned chambers offer an intriguing look into the 19th-century lifestyles of the French nobility and represent the preferences of the time.

A window into the rich cultural past of France and the rest of the world is provided by the wealth of artwork and relics in the Louvre Museum. The Winged Victory of Samothrace, the Mona Lisa, Venus de Milo, and Napoleon III Apartments are just a few of the Louvre's must-see artworks and displays. Anyone who wishes to experience the grandeur and depth of human civilization must tour this famous institution.

Notre-Dame Cathedral and Sainte-Chapelle

Two of the most recognizable church structures in Paris are Notre-Dame Cathedral and Sainte-Chapelle, each of which has a distinctive architectural design and past. We will examine the background and importance of these two magnificent monuments in this chapter.

Cathedral of Notre-Dame

In the center of Paris, there is an ancient Catholic church called Notre-Dame. The cathedral's building process started in 1163 and lasted for more than 200 years. The church is renowned for its elaborate statues, soaring buttresses, stained glass windows, and Gothic design.

The crowning of French monarchs and major religious rituals have taken place at Notre-Dame Cathedral, which has played a significant part in French history.

The church suffered significant harm in a fire in 2019, but repair work is being done to protect this famous site.

Sainte-Chapelle

On Paris's Île de la Cité, Sainte-Chapelle is a Gothic-style church. King Louis IX constructed the church in the 13th century to house his collection of sacred artifacts, which included the Crown of Thorns. The magnificent painted glass windows at Sainte-Chapelle, which show images from the Bible, are well known.

During the French Revolution, the church was destroyed; however, it was subsequently rebuilt. Sainte-Chapelle is still a well-liked location for those interested in ancient building and art today and is accessible to tourists.

Two of the most beautiful sacred structures in Paris are Notre-Dame Cathedral and Sainte-Chapelle, each of which has a distinctive architectural style and background.

While Sainte-Chapelle is an example of ancient art and workmanship, Notre-Dame Cathedral is a representation of French Gothic building and has been significant in French history. Anyone who wishes to experience Paris's grandeur and history must pay these two famous sites a call.

CHAPTER 3

NAVIGATING THE ARRONDISSEMENTS

The Latin Quarter: History and Highlights

On the Left Bank of the Seine River in Paris, there is a thriving and ancient community known as the Latin Quarter. It is renowned for its hippie vibe, buzzing cafés, and charming alleyways. The background and notable features of the Latin Quarter will be covered in this part.

History

The Latin language, which served as the dominant academic tongue during the Middle Ages, gave rise to the moniker "Latin Quarter." Latin was the primary language used by academics and pupils at the Latin Quarter-based University of Paris.

The Latin Quarter in Paris developed into a hub of the city's academic and creative activity during the 19th and 20th centuries.

Numerous well-known authors, painters, and thinkers called it home, among them Ernest Hemingway, James Joyce, and Jean-Paul Sartre.

Highlights

Many important historical and cultural sites can be found in the Latin Quarter. Some of the highlights are as follows:

One of the earliest and most renowned colleges in Europe, Sorbonne University was established in the 13th century. It is a must-see location for anyone interested in the past of schooling and is situated in the center of the Latin Quarter.

Pantheon: Constructed as a cathedral in the 18th century, the Pantheon is a neoclassical structure. Voltaire, Victor Hugo, and Marie Curie are among the notable French people whose graves are now located there.

Jardin du Luxembourg: In the center of the Latin Quarter is the lovely garden known as the Jardin du Luxembourg. It has beautiful ponds, traditional lawns, and waterfalls.

Shakespeare and Company: Since the 1920s, the Latin Quarter has been home to the storied English-language bookshop Shakespeare and Company. In the 20th century, it served as a hub for the meeting of authors and artists in Paris.

For anyone intrigued in Paris's heritage and culture, the Latin Quarter is a must-see location. It is one of the city's most intriguing areas due to its historical monuments, bustling cafés, and artistic vibe. A walk through the Latin Quarter provides insight into the city's lively creative and academic life as well as a trip through Paris's past.

The Marais: Trendy Neighborhood and Attractions

In Paris's third and fourth arrondissements, there is a hip and old district called the Marais. It's renowned for its quaint alleyways, cutting-edge stores, and exciting entertainment. We will examine the Marais's past and charms in this part.

History

In the past, the Marais was a marshy region outside of ancient Paris. It developed into a posh community for the aristocracy in the 16th century, and numerous opulent houses were constructed there. The Marais developed into a hub of Jewish life in Paris during the French Revolution, and it is still home to a flourishing Jewish population today.

The Marais experienced a change in the 20th century and evolved into a fashionable area with an artistic feel. Today, it is one of Paris's most well-liked districts, with a flourishing arts scene, chic shops, and a vibrant nightlife.

Attractions

Numerous historical and cultural landmarks can be found in the Marais. Some of the highlights are as follows:

Musée Carnavalet: The past of Paris is the focus of the Musée Carnavalet. It has displays on Paris' past from ancient times to the present day and is housed in two old houses in the Marais.

Place des Vosges: Situated in the center of the Marais neighborhood, the Place des Vosges is a stunning public plaza. It was constructed in the 17th century, and opulent mansions line its surroundings.

Pompidou Center: Located in the Marais, the Pompidou Center is a showcase of modern art. It is renowned for its distinctive design, which includes open ducting and multicolored pipelines.

Jewish Quarter: The Marais's Jewish Quarter is where you'll find a lot of kosher eateries, Jewish shops, and temples.

Anyone interested in experiencing fashionable Parisian living should explore the Marais. It is one of the city's most intriguing areas thanks to its attractive alleyways, old houses, and thriving arts scene. Everybody can find something to enjoy in the Marais, from its museums to its chic shops. A trip through Paris's past and culture can be had by visiting this thriving area.

Montmartre: The Bohemian District of Paris

The 18th division of Paris contains the historic and artistically inclined neighborhood of Montmartre. It is renowned for its narrow alleyways, quaint cafés, and creative neighborhood. We will examine the past, present, and future of Montmartre in this volume.

History

In the past, Montmartre was a tiny hamlet outside of Paris. It turned into a refuge for artists, authors, and other eccentric types in the late 19th century. Picasso, Toulouse-Lautrec, and Van Gogh were just a few of the well-known painters who resided and worked in Montmartre.

Early in the 20th century, tourists flocked to Montmartre in droves to experience the area's liberal atmosphere and creative community. Montmartre is still a well-liked visitor and artist location today.

Attractions

Numerous historical and cultural landmarks can be found in Montmartre. Some of the highlights are as follows:

The stunning church known as Sacré-Cour is situated atop a slope in Montmartre. One of the most popular tourist destinations in the city, it provides breathtaking vistas of Paris.

Place du Tertre: In this delightful Montmartre plaza, artists market their artwork and create pictures of passersby. It is a fantastic location to discover Montmartre's creative scene.

Moulin Rouge: Located in Montmartre, the Moulin Rouge is a well-known nightclub. It was constructed in 1889 and is renowned for its elaborate performances and can-can performers.

The Musée de Montmartre is a museum that concentrates on the heritage of Montmartre. Exhibits on the liberal way of life in Montmartre in the late 19th and early 20th centuries are on display at this museum, which is housed in a historic home.

Café des Deux Moulins: The Café des Deux Moulins is a delightful café in Montmartre that became well-known thanks to the film "Amélie." It's a wonderful spot to unwind and take in the artistic vibe of the area.

For anyone interested in discovering Paris's eccentric side, Montmartre is a must-visit area. It is one of the most intriguing areas in the city due to its meandering streets, quaint cafés, and creative community. Everyone can enjoy Montmartre's offerings, which range from its historical landmarks to its thriving creative community. A trip through the history and culture of Paris can be had by visiting this eccentric neighborhood.

The Seine River: Cruising and Walking Tours

One of Paris' most recognized and famous characteristics is the Seine River. It is an integral component of Parisian life and meanders through the city's center. The different methods to appreciate the Seine, including sailing and strolling excursions, will be covered in this chapter.

Taking a Seine cruise

A river tour is a fantastic way to experience Paris from a new angle. From intimate supper boats to viewing trips, there are many ways to explore the Seine. Among the well-liked choices are:

One of the most well-known businesses for Seine River excursions is Bateaux-Mouches. They provide a range of excursions, including supper outings, musical events on boats, and viewing visits.

Vedettes de Paris: Vedettes de Paris provides several Seine River excursions, such as Champagne sampling cruises, nighttime meal cruises, and midday viewing visits.

A hop-on, hop-off barge service called Batobus makes calls at a number of sites along the Seine, such as the Eiffel Tower, Notre Dame, and the Louvre Museum.

Pedestrian Tours

A wonderful way to discover Paris and appreciate the majesty of the city is to stroll along the Seine. There are numerous strolling excursions that concentrate on the heritage of the Seine, including:

The Seine River Banks Walk brings you along the Seine River's banks, where you can see many of Paris's well-known attractions, such as the Eiffel Tower, Notre Dame Cathedral, and the Louvre Museum.

Île de la Cité trip: Located in the center of the Seine River, the Île de la Cité is the earliest neighborhood in Paris. This strolling trip brings you there.

The trip involves stops at Sainte-Chapelle and Notre-Dame Cathedral.

The Pont des Arts and the Pont Neuf are two of the most well-known bridges over the Seine that you will traverse on the Paris Bridges Walk. Additionally, you'll see some of Paris's well-known sites from a unique angle.

A wonderful way to experience Paris is to cruise or stroll along the Seine River, which is an integral part of daily living there. The Seine provides something for everyone, whether you opt for an intimate supper boat, a viewing trip, or a relaxing walk along the riverbanks. A trip to Paris would not be complete without admiring this famous river's grandeur and history.

CHAPTER 4

CUISINE CAPITAL

French Food: A Brief History

French food is famous throughout the globe for its refinement, variety, and luxury. The cultural legacy of French cuisine spans millennia, and its cooking customs are steeped in history. In this chapter, we'll briefly examine the development of French cuisine throughout history.

Prior History

French topography, temperature, and area customs have all had a significant impact on the food of the nation. French cooking during the Middle Ages was distinguished by the use of plants, seasonings, and untamed animals. French cookery improved during the Renaissance, with an emphasis on stews and the use of alcohol in the kitchen.

France's Revolution

The way food was made and eaten underwent major change during the French Revolution of 1789. The customary foods that the nobility had previously relished went out of style after they were driven from their position of power. Instead, simpler, more rural meals using regionally obtained products and conventional culinary techniques gained popularity.

High-End Cuisine

French food underwent a time of invention and experimenting in the 19th century. The intricate and refined meals made by French cooks are referred to as "Haute Cuisine." The renowned chef Auguste Escoffier, who defined French cuisine's tenets and laid the groundwork for contemporary cookery methods, ruled the field of culinary arts in France.

French cuisine today

French food is now praised for its variety and originality. Modern French cooks have accepted foreign inspirations, adding fresh products and methods to their country's traditional cuisine.

While staying firmly rooted in the nation's rich culinary history, French food continues to develop and adjust to new culinary trends.

French food reflects the history, topography, and societal customs of the nation. French cuisine has developed over the ages, from the simple meals of the Middle Ages to the elegant and complex inventions of contemporary cooks.

French food is renowned for its innovation, variety, and unmatched quality today and continues to lead the gastronomic globe. Without sampling some of the delectable French cuisine that has turned the nation into a culinary utopia, a trip to Paris would be incomplete.

Classic French Dishes to Try in Paris

No visit to the city of love would be complete without partaking in some traditional French food, which is well renowned for its fine cooking. Here are a few French delicacies you should sample while in Paris:

Duck à Vin

The traditional French meal coq au vin was created in Burgundy, France. It is a meal of poultry that is slowly prepared with red wine, pancetta, shallots, and mushrooms, producing a dish that is delicious and succulent.

Bourguignon beef

Boeuf Bourguignon, another Burgundy-based French staple, is a meat stew made with carrots, shallots, mushrooms, pancetta, and red wine. This warming meal is frequently served with rice or potatoes and is ideal for chilly conditions.

Bourgogne escargots

Burgundy snails, also known as escargots de Bourgogne, are a traditional French entrée. The buttery garlic snails are prepared and presented in their shells, frequently with bread to mop up the mouthwatering sauce.

English Onion Soup

Hearty French onion soup is prepared with sautéed onions, meat stock, and buttered bread and cheese on top. This meal is ideal for a chilly Parisian night.

Croque-Monsieur

The Croque-Monsieur is a traditional French sandwich prepared with ham, cheese, and béchamel sauce. It is a standard in Parisian cafés and is usually given buttered.

Lorraine Quiche

Typically cooked in a flaky shell, quiche Lorraine is a delicious pie prepared with eggs, cream, and bacon. This recipe is ideal for a breakfast or casual supper.

Creme Brulee

Treat is a must-have in Paris because no French dinner is complete without it, and Crème Brûlée is a traditional French treat. A caramelized sugar rim is placed on top of this smooth custard, creating the ideal balance of tastes and textures.

The many gastronomic pleasures that Paris has to offer include these traditional French meals. Parisian cuisine is guaranteed to please any food enthusiast, from flavorful soups to delicious sweets. When visiting Paris, be sure to partake in these traditional French foods for a genuine gastronomic experience.

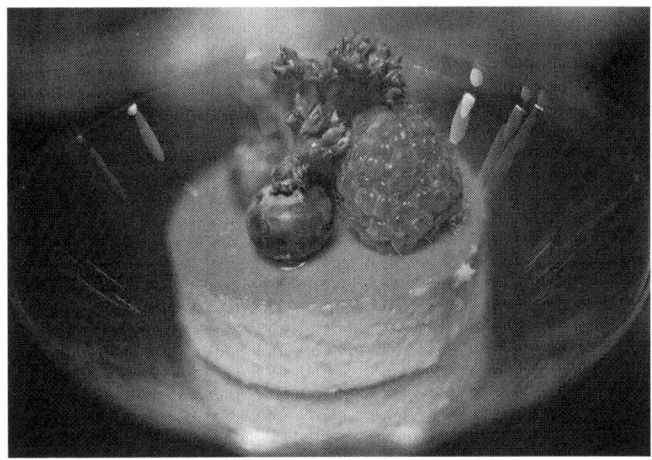

Bistros, Brasseries, and Michelin-Starred Restaurants

Paris is famous for its culinary scene, which features a variety of eating establishments, from classic bistros to upscale Michelin-starred eateries. Here is a list of Paris's various eatery categories:

Bistros

Small, casual eateries called bistros offer classic French fare. They are well-liked by both residents and visitors and frequently have a homey and private ambiance. A fixed menu is usually available at bistros and includes meals like sirloin frites, grilled poultry, and substantial soups.

Brasseries

Bistros and brasseries are comparable, but the former are bigger and more formal. They are well known for their shellfish meals, including clams, mussels, and salmon, and frequently have a busy ambiance. A comprehensive selection with a variety of French and foreign cuisines is usually available at brasseries.

Starred restaurants by Michelin

Numerous Michelin-starred eateries, which are among the finest in the world, can be found in Paris. These eateries provide a great eating experience with outstanding food, flawless service, and classy settings. Restaurants can receive up to three stars from the Michelin Guide depending on the caliber of their fare, service, and atmosphere.

In summation, Paris has something to offer for every flavor and wallet, whether you're searching for a low-key cafe or a luxurious Michelin-starred eatery. Indulge in the gourmet treats of the metropolis for a genuinely memorable eating experience.

Food Markets and Specialty Shops

There are numerous food marketplaces and specialized stores in Paris that sell a broad range of scrumptious and fresh fruits, vegetables, meats, cheeses, bread, sweets, and other delectables. Here are some of Paris's top specialized stores and culinary markets:

Market of Alger

The bustling Marché d'Aligre produce market is situated in Paris's 12th district. In addition to apparel and other products, it has a variety of booths offering fresh fruit, poultry, cheese, and other culinary items. Except for Monday, the market is open every day.

Cler Road

The 7th district of Paris's Rue Cler is a lovely thoroughfare dotted with specialized stores and food vendors. With a variety of bakers, cheese shops, wine shops, and other specialized food stores, it's a well-liked location for connoisseurs.

The Big Eating House in Paris

The 7th district of Paris is home to the luxury cuisine shop La Grande Épicerie de Paris. It provides a broad selection of fine foods, such as cheeses, meats, beverages, and desserts. An eatery and a culinary school are also located in the shop.

Bread Bakery Poilâne

Famous for its handmade bread and sweets, Boulangerie Poilâne is a Parisian patisserie. The Poilâne family continues to operate the bakery, which has been open since 1932. The bakery's distinctive sourdough bread, which is cooked in a wood-fired kiln, is the most well-liked product on the menu.

Quatrehomme Fromagerie

The cheese store Fromagerie Quatrehomme is situated in Paris' 7th district. It provides an extensive selection of French cheeses, such as brie, camembert, and roquefort, in addition to more unusual types. Additionally, the store hosts seminars and lessons on cheese sampling.

The finest fresh vegetables, meats, cheeses, bread, and sweets can be found in a variety of marketplaces and specialized stores throughout Paris, making it a food lover's dream come true. Visit these specialized stores and food marketplaces for a genuine sample of Parisian gastronomy.

CHAPTER 5

HIDDEN GEMS AND LOCAL HANGOUTS

Canal Saint-Martin: A Quirky Neighborhood with Hidden Gems

The northeastern region of Paris contains the lovely and eccentric district of Canal Saint-Martin. It is renowned for its charming waterway, vivacious ambiance, and diverse collection of stores, cafés, and eateries. Here are a few of the undiscovered treasures in this distinctive neighborhood:

Saint-Martin Canal

The neighborhood's focal point and a favorite hangout for both residents and tourists is the waterway. You can relax and take in the scenery, hire a canoe or paddle, or take an unhurried walk along the waterway. The canal's vicinity is filled with quaint cafés and eateries, making it a wonderful location to unwind and observe people.

City of the Figuier

La Cité du Figuier is a secret passageway surrounded by vibrant homes and tiny gardens. It's a wonderful spot to get away from the throngs and a calm and tranquil sanctuary in the middle of the busy neighborhood. A few modest stores and cafés, including a patisserie that has been there for more than a century, are also located in the passageway.

General Comptoir

A distinctive cultural venue and pub called Le Comptoir Général can be found close to the waterway. The location is renowned for its unusual drinks and live music and is furnished with antique furnishings and artwork. It is a fantastic location to experience Parisian culture because it also holds shows, seminars, and other cultural activities.

Prune's Chez

On the canal's shores is a well-known restaurant and tavern called Chez Prune. Since the 1980s, it has become a fixture in the community and is renowned for its laid-back ambiance and traditional French fare. It's a fantastic location for eating or drinking while taking in the canal-side boat traffic.

Saint-Martin Marché

In the center of the area is the outdoor produce market known as Marché Saint-Martin. Along with a few cafés and eateries, it has a variety of booths offering fresh vegetables, meats, cheeses, and other culinary products. You can fill up on supplies for a lunch by the waterway while trying some of the regional food.

Canal Saint-Martin is a quaint and unique community with undiscovered treasures. There is something for everyone in this vibrant and distinctive neighborhood, from the scenic waterway to the multicolored alleys and distinctive stores and eateries.

Along the Canal Saint-Martin, stroll

The center of this area is the Canal Saint-Martin, and strolling along it is one of the finest ways to experience its beauty. Over 4 kilometers of this scenic waterway are surrounded with quaint cafés, tiny bridges, and historic buildings. You can have a lunch on the canal's shores or take an unhurried walk along the water and take in the sights of the passing vessels.

Please go to Le Comptoir Général

A distinctive cultural hub that serves as both a tavern and an eatery is called Le Comptoir Général. Live music, shows, seminars, and other cultural events are presented in this eccentric setting that is furnished with antique furniture and artwork. You can learn about Parisian society there and meet both tourists and residents.

Investigate Rue des Vinaigriers

A delightful thoroughfare with retro shops, antique stores, and little cafés is called Rue des Vinaigriers. It's fun to explore this neighborhood and find interesting stores and regional crafts. For some of the finest coffee and sweets in the area, make sure to visit Maison F.

Chez Prune serves drinks

Since the 1980s, the famous tavern and eatery Chez Prune has been a fixture in the community. Right on the waterway, this bustling area is a wonderful location to unwind with a drink and watch the vessels pass by. Chez Prune is a wonderful place for a quick dinner because it also offers traditional French cuisine.

Visit the Museum of Hunting and Nature

A special exhibit devoted to the craft of shooting and the natural world is called the Musée de la Chasse et de la Nature.

This museum is a wonderful location to learn about the cultural and historical importance of shooting in France and has a varied collection of artwork, artifacts, and natural history exhibits.

Canal Saint-Martin is a distinct and eccentric neighborhood with a wealth of undiscovered treasures.

Everyone will find something to enjoy in this vivacious and dynamic neighborhood of Paris, which includes the scenic waterway, endearing shops, and eccentric cultural spaces.

Parc des Buttes-Chaumont: A Serene Green Space in the City

Parc des Buttes-Chaumont, a secret treasure that is adored by both residents and visitors, is situated northeast of Paris. This tranquil verdant area in the city is the perfect spot to decompress and breathe in some fresh air. Here are some of this lovely park's highlights:

Explore the Gardens

There are many lovely parks in Parc des Buttes-Chaumont, each with special characteristics. The English garden feels more like a natural setting, while the Alpine garden is home to a range of mountain flora. Beautiful city vistas can be found in the Belvédère park, and the suspension bridge makes for a picturesque photo opportunity.

Learn about the Lakes and Waterfalls

The man-made lake and cascade in Parc des Buttes-Chaumont are among its primary draws. This magnificent structure was built in the 19th century and is now the residence of numerous geese and swans. A suspended bridge leads to a tiny island in the lake where you can have a lunch and unwind in the sunshine.

The Activities Are Fun

Visitors can engage in a range of activities at Parc des Buttes-Chaumont. A children's playground, a basketball court, and a sports area are present. Alternatively, you can take a run on one of the jogging paths or hire a canoe and sail around the lake.

Take a trip to the Temple de la Sibylle

On top of a precipice in the park is the stunning building known as the Temple de la Sibylle. This magnificent structure, which provides breathtaking vistas of the park and the surrounding metropolis, was modeled after the Temple of Vesta in Tivoli, Italy.

Unwind and Relish

The tranquil ambiance at Parc des Buttes-Chaumont is one of its finest features. This tranquil urban park provides a peaceful haven from the noise and activity of Paris. On the lawn, you can unwind, read a novel, or just take in the lovely scenery.

Paris's Parc des Buttes-Chaumont is a secret treasure that provides a tranquil and calm escape from the city. This lovely park is a must-visit for anyone wanting to experience the natural grandeur of Paris, whether you want to wander through the grounds, learn about the cascades and lakes, or just decompress and enjoy.

Promenade Plantée: Paris's Secret Garden Walkway

Paris's "secret garden" is frequently referred to as the Promenade Plantée, also known as the Coulée green René-Dumont. Built on an old railroad track, this stunning raised park extends more than three miles from Bastille to the Bois de Vincennes.

Here are some Promenade Plantée highlights:

Specialized Architecture

The Promenade Plantée's distinctive design is one of its most eye-catching characteristics. The park has a unique and peculiar appearance because the pathway is constructed over an elevated railway line and the original bridge has been maintained. You'll pass by a variety of lovely flora and blossoms along the route, as well as passageways and bridges.

Beautiful Views

Beautiful vistas of the city, including the Bastille district, the Viaduc des Arts, and the Jardin de Reuilly, are available from the Promenade Plantée. You'll have the impression that you're strolling above the city as you stroll along the high route, and there are stunning vistas everywhere you look.

Natural Grace

Roses, lavender, and jasmine are just a few of the lovely flora and blooms that can be found in the park. As you stroll through the park, you'll also notice a variety of plants and bushes that create a calm and unwinding atmosphere.

Inspiration for the Arts

Thanks to its distinctive design and breathtaking vistas, the Promenade Plantée has become a well-liked destination for artists and photographers. A wonderful location to find up-and-coming artists is the Viaduc des Arts, which runs adjacent to the promenade and is home to a variety of art shops and studios.

Exercise and Relaxation

Both residents and visitors enjoy the tranquil refuge provided by the Promenade Plantée from the hubbub of the city. This particular garden path is a must-visit for anyone looking for a distinctive and tranquil experience in Paris, whether you're looking to take an unhurried saunter, go for an exercise, or simply rest and appreciate the natural beauty.

Finally, the Promenade Plantée is a secret Parisian treasure that provides a singular and tranquil escape from the city. Anyone seeking to discover Paris's undiscovered gems must explore this lovely garden path with its distinctive design, breathtaking vistas, and natural beauty.

Village Saint-Paul: A Labyrinth of Antique Shops and Art Galleries

Located in the Marais neighborhood of Paris, Village Saint-Paul is a secret treasure that draws tourists in with its maze of vintage stores and art galleries. One of the few locations in the city that has managed to maintain its genuine character, the neighborhood emanates an old-world appeal.

Here are some of Village Saint-Paul's highlights:

An Ideal Shopping Place

More than 200 antique stores and studios can be found in Village Saint-Paul, offering everything from rare books to modern art to rare books, antique furnishings, and retro jewelry. In this lovely area, visitors can be sure to discover something distinctive and one-of-a-kind. It's simple to lose an entire day perusing the stores with such a huge variety of goods on sale.

A dynamic museum

The structures have been meticulously maintained to maintain their original character, and the region has a long past that goes back to the Middle Ages. The building's design combines Renaissance, Gothic, and Classical elements. The charming features of this living museum include the winding cobblestone streets, secret gardens, and ivy-covered walls.

Creative Haven

The innovative ambiance of Village Saint-Paul attracts designers and artists from all over the globe. The neighborhood exudes a creative atmosphere, with shops displaying the creations of both well-known and up-and-coming artists. Many vintage stores have original statues and drawings on exhibit, demonstrating that creative expression is not just found in galleries.

Quaint restaurants and cafes

A haven for chefs as well as vintage and art aficionados can be found in Village Saint-Paul. There are several quaint cafés and restaurants in the area that serve a range of delectable French food, from traditional crepes to contemporary hybrid meals. The cafés' external sitting spaces make for the ideal place to unwind and observe the passing scenery.

A Calm Escape

Despite being in the middle of the Marais neighborhood, not many visitors are familiar with Village Saint-Paul. Visitors can find peace here as they avoid the busy throngs of the metropolis. With so many silent nooks to discover, the region is the ideal place for an unhurried walk thanks to its tranquil ambiance.

Village Saint-Paul is a must-see location for anyone interested in antiques, art, or a distinctive Parisian experience. The region is perfect for a relaxed day excursion because of its rich heritage, creative atmosphere, and quaint cafés and eateries.

CHAPTER 6

ROMANCE IN PARIS

Romantic Walks: Strolls Along the Seine and Beyond

There is an excellent reason why Paris is referred to as the "City of Love." Couples should visit the city because of its charming alleyways and spectacular building because it has an amorous atmosphere. The most charming things to do in Paris are walks with your special someone. Here are some of the city's most amorous strolls:

Next to the Seine River

A walk along the Seine is a must-do activity when in Paris. The waterway runs through the center of the city and provides breathtaking vistas of famous buildings like the Notre-Dame Cathedral and the Eiffel Tower. An amorous stroll along the riverbanks would be ideal because of the scenic bridges, classy quays, and endearing cafés that line the banks.

By way of Montmartre

The delightful district of Montmartre is renowned for its creative heritage and free-spirited atmosphere. You can discover secret gardens, charming bistros, and breathtaking city vistas by meandering through its tiny, cobblestoned streets and alleys. The journey to the Basilica of the Sacred Heart of Paris, which provides stunning panorama views of the city, is the highlight of the stroll.

Luxembourg Gardens

The Luxembourg Gardens are a calm haven in the middle of the city that provides a peaceful haven from the busy throngs. The courtyard is the ideal place for an intimate stroll thanks to its verdant grass, lovely waterfalls, and carefully manicured bushes. The grounds are filled with seats and chairs, making them the ideal spot to relax and take in the landscape.

Encompassing the Canal Saint-Martin

The beautiful canal that meanders through the northeast of the city is called the Canal Saint-Martin. You will pass delightful footbridges, busy cafés, and cute shops as you stroll along the canal's tree-lined banks. The vibrant ambiance of the area makes it the ideal location for a romantic walk.

By way of the Marais

Paris's fashionable Marais district is well-known for its magnificent building, congested streets, and quaint cafés. You can find secret gardens, art galleries, and specialty stores by strolling through the area's winding, cobblestone streets. When the streets are illuminated at night, the Marais is particularly seductive because it has a mystical atmosphere.

Finally, there are many amorous excursions in Paris, each with a special appeal. A romance walk is the ideal way to experience the majesty and appeal of the city with your significant other, whether you decide to saunter along the Seine River or through the charming neighborhood of Montmartre.

Classic Parisian Experiences for Couples

One of the most beautiful cities in the world is Paris, the City of Love. In Paris, couples can do anything from stroll along the Seine River to take in the breathtaking architecture and savor fine cuisine. The following traditional Parisian activities are ideal for couples:

Take a Seine River sunset tour: A Seine River sunset cruise is a classic Parisian adventure. You'll be able to see some of the city's most well-known structures as you glide down the river, including the Eiffel Tower, Notre-Dame Cathedral, and the Louvre Museum. Many businesses provide evening cruises that combine a delectable meal with breathtaking scenery.

Kiss each other at the summit of the Eiffel Tower: The Eiffel Tower is one of the most famous and romantic landmarks in the world. As you and your partner ascend the structure, exchange kisses and take in the breathtaking views of the city below.

One of Paris' most stunning green areas, the Luxembourg Gardens are a wonderful place to have a picnic. Find a secluded location to unwind and enjoy each other's company after packing a picnic box with some wine and cheese.

Take a romantic stroll through Montmartre: With its winding cobblestone streets, quaint cafés, and breathtaking city views, Montmartre is one of Paris's most endearing districts. Wander the area on a date and take in the stunning street art and architecture.

Enjoy a romantic supper by candlelight at a Michelin-starred establishment: Paris is renowned for its exceptional dining scene, and there are many Michelin-starred establishments to choose from. Spend a romantic evening with your significant other enjoying some of the best food the city has to offer over a candlelit supper.

Rent a vintage bike to tour the city, then tour the area with your special someone. It's an exciting and different way to see the city, and as you fly past its famous sites, you'll imagine yourself in a love story.

Attend a ballet or opera at the Palais Garnier: With its elaborate design and breathtaking performances, the Palais Garnier is one of the world's most beautiful opera houses. For a truly magical evening, get dressed up and take your special someone to a dance or opera.

There are countless opportunities for partners to make priceless memories in the romantic and charming city of Paris. Paris offers something for every couple to appreciate, whether they want to spend a romantic evening at home or have an exciting day out.

Best Romantic Restaurants and Bars

Couples seeking a romantic evening will find many restaurants and bars in Paris, which is renowned for being a romantic city. Here are some of the top places for a romance getaway:

The Michelin-starred Le Jules Verne restaurant is situated on the second level of the Eiffel Tower and features a gourmet French cuisine in addition to stunning views of the city.

Le Comptoir du Relais is a cozy Saint-Germain-des-Prés bistro that's ideal for a special supper. The menu offers traditional French cuisine, and the setting is welcoming and friendly.

La Maison Rose - This charming pink restaurant is a favorite among both residents and visitors and is tucked away in the Montmartre neighborhood. The outdoor seating is ideal for a summer evening, and the cuisine is straightforward but delicious.

Another hidden treasure near the Eiffel Tower, Les Ombres serves up a contemporary French menu and boasts a breathtaking view of the city at night.

Bar Hemingway - Located in the Ritz hotel, this traditional Parisian bar is renowned for its refined ambiance and skillfully crafted cocktails. the ideal location for a nightcap following a special meal.

Le Bar du Plaza Athénée is a must-visit for lovers seeking a posh evening. It is located in the venerable Plaza Athénée hotel. The drinks are creative, and the setting is upscale and fashionable.

Hidden behind a taqueria, Candelaria is a hip bar with a laid-back atmosphere in the Marais. The inventive drinks and the cozy setting are ideal for a romantic evening out.

Le Perchoir is a rooftop bar in the 11th arrondissement that provides breathtaking city views in addition to a laid-back and chic ambiance. The ideal place to enjoy a refreshment with your significant other in the summer.

Overall, couples seeking a unique evening out will find many romantic restaurants and bars in Paris. There is something for everyone to appreciate, from trendy speakeasies to Michelin-starred restaurants.

Exploring Paris's Romantic Past and Present

It's understandable why Paris is referred to as the "City of Love" throughout the globe. Paris has long been a center of romance thanks to its winding streets, ancient buildings, quaint cafes, and parks. The best methods to discover Paris's romantic past and present are listed below:

Walk Through Montmartre - This 18th arrondissement hilltop community is renowned for its bohemian atmosphere and quaint alleyways. Artists like Picasso and Van Gogh frequented the area, and today it is teeming with cafés, art galleries, and swanky establishments like the famed Moulin Rouge.

Visit the Palais-Royal, a historic mansion in the center of Paris that was once the scene of much romantic intrigue. It was where Napoleon and Josephine held their private talks there, and it was also the location of Coco Chanel's first store.

The grounds are now a serene location for a passionate stroll.

Discover the Marais - The Place des Vosges, a lovely park surrounded by old buildings, is just one romantic location in this hip district in the 4th arrondissement. It's the ideal place for an exploration-filled day with your significant other because it also has a ton of cafés, shops, and art galleries.

Walk along the Seine River - From the famous Pont des Arts bridge to the quaint Île Saint-Louis island, the banks of the Seine are full of romantic locations. Take a stroll along the river and pause at one of the numerous cafés or bookshops to admire the scenery.

Visit the Musée Rodin, which is located in a beautiful sculpture garden and a historic mansion. The works of Rodin are certain to arouse emotions of passion and love, making it the ideal location for a romantic afternoon.

In general, Paris is a romantic city with a long heritage of love and romance. Discovering the city's history and present together is a wonderful way to share Paris' magic with your special someone.

CHAPTER 7

ART AND CULTURE

Paris Museums and Art Galleries

Paris is regarded as one of the world's intellectual capitals, and its museums and art galleries are evidence of this claim. There is a museum or gallery in Paris that will fit your interests, whether they are in classical art, modern art, or something in between. Some of the top places to go are listed below:

The Louvre Museum: With a collection that covers more than 9,000 years of human history, the Louvre is one of the most well-known museums in the world. The Winged Victory of Samothrace, the Mona Lisa, and the Venus de Milo are a few of its most well-known displays.

A former railway station now houses the impressive Impressionist and Post-Impressionist art collection known as the Musée d'Orsay, which includes works by Monet, Van Gogh, and Degas.

The Centre Georges Pompidou, a museum of modern and contemporary art, is renowned for its eye-catching design and exterior pipes and ducts in vibrant colors. There are pieces inside by artists like Warhol, Matisse, and Picasso.

Musée Rodin: This museum showcases the creations of renowned French sculptor Auguste Rodin and includes both interior and outdoor exhibits.

Musée de l'Orangerie: This remarkable collection of Impressionist and Post-Impressionist artwork, which is housed in the Tuileries Garden, includes Monet's well-known Water Lilies.

Pablo Picasso's artwork is the focus of the Musée Picasso, which has over 5,000 of his pieces on exhibit.

The Musée de l'Armée, housed in the old military hospital Les Invalides, is home to a sizable collection of artifacts and military history, including Napoleon's tomb.

The non-Western art and artifacts on display at the Musée du Quai Branly come from civilizations in Africa, Asia, Oceania, and the Americas.

The Middle Ages to the present are represented in the displays at the Musée Carnavalet, a museum devoted to the history of Paris.

The Fondation Louis Vuitton is a modern art museum with a striking glass and steel exterior that was created by Frank Gehry. Contemporary painters like Yayoi Kusama and Jeff Koons have pieces inside.

These museums and art galleries are must-see locations during your trip to the City of Light, whether you're an art enthusiast or just want to learn more about Paris's rich cultural history.

Art Nouveau and Art Deco Architecture in Paris

With a long heritage of architectural styles, Paris is renowned for its stunning architecture. Art Nouveau and Art Deco, two of the most well-known architectural movements in the city, are praised for their distinctive characteristics and aesthetic appeal. Here is a deeper look at Paris's Art Nouveau and Art Deco buildings.

Art Nouveau Construction

The late 19th century saw the emergence of the Art Nouveau style, which is translated from the French as "new art" and thrived until the First World War. It was distinguished by the use of organic shapes, curved lines, and complex designs. Hector Guimard, who created several recognizable metro entrances in the city, including the well-known "dragonfly" entrances, popularized the form in Paris.

The Castel Béranger by Hector Guimard, which is regarded as the first Art Nouveau structure in the world, is one of the other noteworthy examples of Art Nouveau architecture in Paris. Intricate ironwork, stained glass windows, sinuous lines, and an asymmetrical design are all features of the structure.

The Maison de l'Art Nouveau, which Samuel Bing created as a gallery to display Art Nouveau art and architecture, is another well-known Art Nouveau structure in Paris.

The structure has a lovely façade with a central panel showing a lady holding a peacock feather and a wrought-iron balcony.

Art Deco construction

Contrarily, Art Deco, which began to appear in the 1920s and persisted through the start of World War II, was distinguished by its geometric forms, vivid colors, and streamlined designs. The materials used in industrial manufacturing and the age of the machine had a big impact on the style.

The Palais de Chaillot, which was constructed for the 1937 World's Fair, is just one of the famous structures in Paris that feature Art Deco design. The structure has two curved wings, a central tower, and elaborate carvings and reliefs on the exterior.

The Théâtre des Champs-Élysées, another well-known Art Deco structure in Paris, was created by Auguste Perret and has a simple, elegant façade with striking geometric designs and a central tower.

The theater's interior is also styled in the Art Deco manner, with streamlined designs and opulent materials.

Art Nouveau and Art Deco are just two of the many architectural styles that can be found all over the city of Paris, which honors its rich history and culture. The distinctive characteristics of these styles continue to motivate and enthrall tourists to Paris, from the iconic metro entrances to the largest buildings.

Famous French Artists and Their Works

Paris has long been a hub for art and culture, and France has long produced many significant artists. French art has had a significant influence on the world of art, from the impressionists to the modernists. Some well-known French artists and their creations are listed below:

Claude Monet: Known for his impressionist technique, Monet frequently portrayed the splendor of nature in his works. His "Water Lilies" collection of paintings, which depict the serenity of a pond in his garden, is among his most well-known creations.

Despite being of Dutch descent, Vincent van Gogh lived the majority of his professional life in France and was greatly influenced by the French impressionist movement. His vivid and emotive works, like "Starry Night," are now regarded as some of the most recognizable in the entire globe.

Henri Matisse, a pioneer of the Fauvism movement, is renowned for his daring use of color and uncomplicated shapes. His paintings of dancers, "Dance," and "The Red Studio," which highlights his use of color, are some of his most well-known pieces.

Pablo Picasso: Despite being of Spanish descent, Picasso lived the majority of his professional life in France and rose to prominence within the modernist movement. He is credited with producing some of the most important works of the 20th century, including "Les Demoiselles d'Avignon" and "Guernica."

Edgar Degas was an expert at depicting motion and movement in his works. His paintings of ballet performers, such as "The Dance Class" and "The Rehearsal," are perhaps best known.

Auguste Rodin: Among the most significant artists of the 19th century, Rodin created "The Thinker" and "The Kiss," which are now regarded as two of the most recognizable works of art.

Georges Seurat: Seurat is renowned for his use of pointillism, a painting method in which a picture is made up of tiny dots of color. "A Sunday Afternoon on the Island of La Grande Jatte," his most well-known piece, shows Parisians having a good time in the park.

These are just a few of the numerous well-known French painters who have had a profound influence on the art world. There are many museums and galleries in Paris where visitors can view the artists' creations up close and develop a better understanding of the city's rich artistic history.

Performing Arts and Festivals in Paris

Festivals and venues for the performing arts are abundant in Paris. The city has a thriving performing arts scene that draws both residents and visitors. It includes everything from classical music to modern dance, theater to opera. The following are some of the best performing arts events and gatherings in Paris:

One of the most well-known opera companies in the world, the Opéra de Paris has two locations: The Palais Garnier and the Opéra Bastille. Because of its historical and cultural importance, the Palais Garnier, with its elaborate and opulent interiors, is a must-see.

Opera, theater, and dance events are held at the Théâtre du Châtelet, which is a venue in the center of Paris. It is renowned for its varied programming, which includes both traditional and modern productions.

Event d'Automne: From September to December each year, the Festival d'Automne hosts an arts event. The festival draws artists from all over the globe and offers a wide variety of performances, including theater, dance, and visual arts.

Paris Jazz Festival: This jazz music festival features performances by both domestic and foreign artists each summer in the Parc Floral de Paris.

Fête de la Musique: Every year on the summer solstice, a free music event called the Fête de la Musique is held. Throughout the city, the event will hold concerts and performances in parks, streets, and other public areas.

Paris Fashion Week is a bi-annual event that features the newest fashion trends from top designers and fashion companies. Paris is one of the four major fashion centers of the world.

Festival d'Avignon: Just outside of Paris in the city of Avignon, there is a famous performing arts festival known as the Festival d'Avignon.

Performances of theater, dance, and music by both well-known and up-and-coming artists are featured at the event.

Musée d'Orsay: This museum is home to a sizable collection of Impressionist and Post-Impressionist works of art. Monet, Manet, and Van Gogh's works, among others, are among the magnificent selection of artworks in the museum.

One of the world's biggest collections of modern and contemporary art is housed in the Centre Pompidou, a museum of contemporary art. The museum's striking and avant-garde building, created by Renzo Piano and Richard Rogers, is well-known.

The Fondation Louis Vuitton is a museum of modern art with a collection of works by both well-known and up-and-coming artists. Art lovers must tour the museum, which is housed in a striking building created by Frank Gehry.

CHAPTER 8

SHOPPING AND FASHION

Parisian Fashion: A Brief History

With a lengthy history and a reputation for haute couture and upscale clothing, Paris has long been regarded as one of the world's fashion capitals. Since the 19th century, the city's fashion business has been growing and has contributed significantly to the development of the global fashion scene.

Paris rose to prominence as a fashion hub in the early 19th century thanks to a booming textile industry and a rise in the popularity of ready-to-wear apparel. The mass production of apparel made possible by the invention of the sewing machine in the middle of the nineteenth century opened up fashion to a wider audience.

Parisian fashion designers started to position themselves as industry titans in the early 20th century. One of the most famous designers of the era,

Coco Chanel invented a more relaxed, comfortable look that was both wearable and stylish.

Paul Poiret and Jeanne Lanvin were two other prominent fashion designers of the time.

Haute couture flourished in the 1940s and 1950s, when Parisian fashion companies like Christian Dior, Yves Saint Laurent, and Pierre Balmain came to represent elegance and luxury. With their cutting-edge designs and use of pricey materials, these designers changed fashion and still have an impact on it today.

Paris Fashion Week is one of the most significant occasions in the fashion business, taking place twice a year in January and September. It draws fashion editors, celebrities, and fashion enthusiasts from all over the globe and features the most recent collections from top fashion designers.

Numerous renowned fashion organizations, such as the Musée de la Mode et du Textile and the Musée Yves Saint Laurent Paris, are located in the city's fashion district.

These institutions display the evolution of French fashion as well as the creations of some of the greatest designers in history.

As more designers from various backgrounds and cultures make their imprint on the industry, Parisian fashion has recently become more inclusive and varied. The city's fashion culture continues to be at the top of the field and to influence designers and fashion enthusiasts worldwide.

Fashion Boutiques and Department Stores

For good reason, Paris is regarded as one of the world's fashion capitals. Numerous of the most prestigious fashion houses and designers in the world have their offices in this city, which has long been a center of creativity and innovation in the fashion industry.

There is no shortage of fashion in Paris, from high fashion to street wear. The following are some of the top clothing stores and boutiques to visit while you are there:

One of the most well-known department stores in the city is Galeries Lafayette, which is situated in the center of Paris. The store offers both more affordable options and a wide selection of high-end fashion labels like Chanel, Dior, and Saint Laurent. Visitors can enjoy the building's stunning Art Nouveau architecture in addition to shopping there.

Le Bon Marché is a well-known department store in Paris and has been a part of the city's landscape since 1852. The store is renowned for its high-end fashion selections, which include designer labels like Givenchy and Louis Vuitton. Additionally, it has a section of gourmet foods and a range of home goods.

For those who enjoy fashion, Colette in the first arrondissement is a must-visit store. Colette has a café, gallery space, and a carefully chosen assortment of designer apparel, accessories, and beauty products.

Merci is a concept store that combines goods for the home, fashion, and design. Merci is situated in the chic Marais neighborhood. Along with a café and a bookstore, the shop offers a distinctive selection of clothing and accessories.

Another renowned department store in Paris, Printemps is renowned for its opulent shopping atmosphere and stunning Art Deco design.

High-end brands and more budget-friendly options are both available in the store's extensive selection of fashion items.

The Broken Arm is a trendy store with a café, gallery space, and a mix of high-end and up-and-coming fashion brands in the Haut Marais neighborhood.

Chanel – A trip to the flagship Chanel store on Rue Cambon would not be complete without one. The shop offers a variety of accessories and fragrances in addition to the newest collections from the renowned fashion house.

Maison Margiela - This fashion house has a store in the Marais district and is well-known for its avant-garde designs and disassembled clothing. Men's and women's clothing and accessories are available in the store.

Hermès - For fans of high fashion, the Hermès flagship store on Rue du Faubourg Saint-Honoré is a must-see. The shop sells the recognizable clothing, leather goods, and silk scarves from the brand.

A.P.C. is a minimalist clothing line with a store in the Marais district that sells its iconic denim and other classic items.

Vintage and Second-Hand Shopping in Paris

Any fashion enthusiast should not skip out on the unique experience of vintage and used goods shopping in Paris. There is something for everyone in the city's many vintage and second-hand stores, from designer items to one-of-a-kind finds.

The Marais neighborhood, which has many shops selling vintage and used clothing, shoes, and accessories, is one of the most well-liked places to go vintage buying. These stores are excellent choices for anyone searching for high-end items at a fraction of their original cost because many of them concentrate on high-end designer brands.

The Marché aux Puces de Saint-Ouen, one of the biggest flea marketplaces in the world, is another must-see place for vintage and used shopping. Over 2,500 stalls with everything from vintage clothing to antique furnishings are available for shoppers to peruse here.

There are several shops in Paris that specialize in vintage and used clothing for those seeking a more curated experience. These stores are a fantastic option for anyone looking to add a distinctive touch to their wardrobe because they offer carefully chosen items that are frequently in excellent condition.

Paris is home to many consignment stores where customers can find gently used designer apparel and accessories at a cost in addition to vintage and second-hand stores. These stores are a fantastic option for anyone who wants to keep up with the most recent fashions because they frequently stock items that are current and on-trend.

When it comes to vintage and used shopping, Paris has something for everyone, whether you're an experienced vintage shopper or simply searching for a distinctive item to add to your wardrobe.

With so many choices, it's simple to spend a whole day perusing the city's many markets and shops, discovering undiscovered treasures and one-of-a-kind finds along the way.

Parisian Fashion and Style Tips

Many tourists are anxious to experience Paris' sartorial culture because the city is known for its fashion and style. Here are some pointers for getting the classic Parisian appearance:

Invest in high-quality basics because quality is always preferred over abundance in French fashion. Invest in a few well-made, classic pieces that go with everything in your closet.

Accept the classics: The trench coat, the Breton shirt, and the little black dress are among the ageless items that are at the foundation of French fashion. When buying in Paris, keep an eye out for these timeless items.

Maintain a neutral color scheme: Black, white, blue, and beige are common neutrals among Parisians. This is not to say that you can't add a splash of color here and there, but try to keep your color scheme simple generally.

Parisians are renowned for their naturally chic accessorizing, so accessorize with care. Choose a few well-made, understated items, such as a leather purse, a silk scarf, and a pair of traditional sunglasses.

Parisians are experts at dressing appropriately for any situation. Make sure you are dressed properly whether you are going to a brunch, a fancy dinner, or a museum.

Examine the fit carefully because French fashion is all about elongating, tailored shapes. Make sure your attire is comfortable and highlights your best features.

Don't be afraid to combine expensive and inexpensive things; Parisians are experts at doing this. Spending money on a few essential pieces is okay, but you should also feel free to combine them with more reasonably priced pieces.

Never forget that conviction is the key component of Parisian style. Don't be afraid to take chances and attempt new things; wear what makes you feel good.

CHAPTER 9

OUTDOOR ADVENTURES

Parks and Gardens in Paris

Beautiful parks and gardens in Paris are well-known for providing a tranquil haven from the busy metropolis. The best parks and gardens in Paris are listed below:

The exquisite Jardin des Tuileries was built in the 16th century for Catherine de' Medici and is situated between the Louvre and Place de la Concorde. It has fountains, statues, and lovely landscaping.

Luxembourg Gardens: With its fountains, trimmed grounds, and tree-lined promenades, this sizable park in the middle of the city provides a tranquil haven. It's a well-liked location for relaxing, running, and picnics.

One of the biggest parks in the capital is Parc des Buttes-Chaumont, a hilly park in northeastern Paris. It offers breathtaking views of the metropolis as well as a lake, waterfalls, and a grotto.

Lakes, gardens, and woods are all part of the expansive Bois de Boulogne park, which is located on the city's western outskirts. It's a well-liked location for outdoor pursuits like biking and boating.

The vast Parc de la Villette in northeastern Paris is home to a scientific museum, a concert venue, and a number of gardens and outdoor areas. With kids, it's a fantastic location to explore.

The 8th arrondissement's elegant Parc Monceau is home to a number of sculptures, fountains, and architectural details. It's a well-liked location for resting and jogging.

Square du Vert-Galant: Situated on the westernmost point of the Île de la Cité, this small park provides breathtaking views of the Seine and the neighboring urban landscape. It's a wonderful location for a picnic or romantic walk.

There are numerous other parks in Paris besides these ones, from the ancient Parc des Princes to the contemporary Parc de la Butte-du-Chapeau-Rouge.

There is a park or garden in Paris for every passion, so visit one today.

Biking and Hiking Trails in and Around the City

There is no better way to experience Paris, a city renowned for its charm and beauty, than by going for a leisurely bike ride or a breathtaking walk through some of its many parks and natural areas. The top bicycling and hiking routes in and around Paris are listed below.

Miles of paved and unpaved paths are available for biking and hiking in the Bois de Boulogne, a sizable park on the western outskirts of Paris. A big lake, a number of eateries, and a botanical garden are also located there.

The expansive Bois de Vincennes park, which is on the eastern outskirts of Paris, is ideal for lengthy bike or hike rides. It has several lakes, a zoo, a botanical park, and a castle from the Middle Ages.

From the Bastille to the Bois de Vincennes, the Coulée Verte is a 4.7 km long scenic route for bicyclists and pedestrians. It's an excellent method to enjoy the city's parks without being in the traffic.

The 19th arrondissement's hilly Parc des Buttes-Chaumont has a number of beautiful paths for bicycling and hiking. A sizable lagoon and a well-known suspension bridge are also located there.

The 19th arrondissement's Parc de la Villette is a sizable park with a scientific museum, several themed gardens, and a venue for outdoor concerts. There are numerous hiking and biking paths there as well.

The 14th arrondissement's Parc Montsouris is renowned for its picturesque lake, undulating slopes, and tree-lined pathways. The area is well-liked by joggers and pedestrians.

The Forêt de Fontainebleau is a well-known hiking and climbing location that is located about an hour south of Paris. It has miles of paths that wind through rocky gorges, sand dunes, and thick forests.

Promenade des Deux Rives: This 15 km bike and pedestrian route follows the Seine's banks and connects Paris and Ivry-sur-Seine. It provides breathtaking views of the waterway and the skyline of the city.

There are numerous trails and natural areas in Paris to discover whether you prefer to bike or hike. So put on your walking shoes or hire a bike and head out to see the city's charm and grandeur for yourself.

River and Canal Activities: Kayaking, Boating, and More

The River Seine and the Canal Saint-Martin are just two of the lovely waterways in the metropolis of Paris. These rivers can be enjoyed in a variety of ways, including kayaking, boating, and other activities.

Both locals and visitors enjoy kayaking as a pastime. Many businesses provide guided kayaking tours of the Seine, providing tourists with a distinctive view of the city.

These excursions can last anywhere from an hour to several hours and frequently halt at well-known sites like the Eiffel Tower and Notre-Dame Cathedral.

Another well-liked activity on the Seine is boating, and several businesses give sightseeing cruises. These excursions, which typically last an hour, provide a tranquil way to view the city from a different angle. A romantic way to spend an evening in Paris is to take one of the many companies that offer evening cruises that include supper and drinks.

On the Seine, paddleboat accommodations are also offered for those who prefer a more active experience. These can be an enjoyable way to get some exercise while independently exploring the river.

Another waterway with interesting events is the Canal Saint-Martin. Taking a boat tour of the canal, which takes guests through several locks and under several bridges, is a well-liked choice. The journey presents a distinctive view of the city's past and present.

Stand-up paddleboards can be rented for those who prefer a more active time on the canal. This can be an exciting and difficult way to tour the canal and get a new perspective on the city.

Overall, visitors can engage in a diversity of activities along Paris's waterways. There are many choices to choose from, whether you want a leisurely boat cruise or an exciting kayaking adventure.

Day Trips to Natural Wonders Near Paris

Paris is not only surrounded by lovely towns and quaint villages, but it is also close to numerous natural marvels that are worthwhile day trips from the city. Here are some natural areas you can visit close to Paris:

Gardens at Château de Versailles: The gardens at Château de Versailles are among the most exquisite and meticulously maintained in the world. Take a day to stroll through the grounds, observing the fountains and the lovely plants and trees.

Near the city of Paris, the Fontainebleau Forest is a fantastic location to go hiking and rock climbing. Numerous magnificent castles, including the Château de Fontainebleau, can be found in the woodland.

Giverny: Giverny is a tiny hamlet about an hour's drive from Paris. It is renowned for its lovely gardens, which served as the model for many of Claude Monet's most well-known works of art.

Off the shore of Normandy is the breathtaking island of Mont Saint-Michel. The island is encircled by a lovely harbor and is home to an old abbey.

The Château de Chantilly is a stunning palace that was once the residence of the Duke of Aumale. It is only 30 miles north of Paris. The castle houses an art museum and is surrounded by lovely grounds.

The breathtaking Château de Vaux-le-Vicomte is just 35 miles southeast of Paris. Built in the 17th century, the castle is encircled by lovely grounds and fountains.

Just 50 miles north of Paris is the medieval fortress known as Château de Pierrefonds. The TV program Merlin used it as a filming site. It was constructed in the fourteenth century.

A small hamlet called Auvers-sur-Oise is just thirty minutes from Paris. It is well-known for housing Vincent van Gogh's ultimate resting place and serving as the location of a museum devoted to his life and work.

These breathtaking natural attractions close to Paris provide a tranquil escape from the hubbub of the city. They provide a chance to experience the rich history and culture of the area as well as the French landscape.

CHAPTER 10

BEYOND THE CITY LIMITS

Palace of Versailles: A Day Trip to the Lavish Royal Residence

The Palace of Versailles is an iconic attraction located just a short distance outside of Paris. This lavish royal residence was originally built by Louis XIII in the early 17th century, but it was Louis XIV who transformed it into the stunning palace we know today.

The Palace of Versailles is one of the most popular day trips from Paris, and it's easy to see why. From the ornate architecture to the beautifully landscaped gardens, there's plenty to see and do here.

Visiting the Palace of Versailles is like stepping back in time to the days of the French monarchy. The palace itself is a magnificent example of Baroque architecture, with grand halls, intricate carvings, and gilded accents.

Visitors can take a guided tour of the palace to learn more about its history and see some of the most famous rooms, such as the Hall of Mirrors.

The palace's gardens are equally impressive, covering over 800 hectares of land. The gardens are meticulously landscaped, with fountains, sculptures, and even a canal. Visitors can rent a bike or a golf cart to explore the gardens at their leisure, or they can take a guided tour to learn more about the history of this beautiful space.

Aside from the palace and gardens, there are several other attractions to see at Versailles. The Grand Trianon, a smaller palace located on the grounds, is another popular attraction, as is the Petit Trianon, a small chateau that was once home to Marie Antoinette. The Queen's Hamlet, a small village built to look like a rustic farm, is also worth a visit.

Getting to the Palace of Versailles is easy from Paris. Visitors can take the RER C train from the city center to Versailles, which takes about 45 minutes. Once at the station, it's a short walk to the palace.

It's important to note that the palace can get very busy, especially during peak tourist season, so it's a good idea to book tickets in advance to skip the lines.

In conclusion, the Palace of Versailles is a must-see attraction for anyone visiting Paris. With its stunning architecture, beautiful gardens, and fascinating history, it's a destination that is sure to leave a lasting impression. Whether you're a history buff or just looking for a beautiful day trip, the Palace of Versailles is well worth a visit.

Champagne Tasting in Reims and Épernay

What better location to sample Champagne, one of France's most well-known exports, than in the region where it is produced? Just a short train journey from Paris are the towns of Reims and Épernay, which are situated in the center of the Champagne region. What you should know before sampling Champagne in Reims and Épernay is as follows:

Champagne Houses: Reims and Épernay are home to a number of Champagne houses, including some of the most well-known worldwide brands like Moet & Chandon, Veuve Clicquot, and Pommery. Many of these estates allow visitors to take cellar tours and taste their various blends while learning how Champagne is made.

Champagne houses aren't the only places where tourists can taste different Champagnes from various producers; there are also a lot of independent tasting rooms.

These spaces frequently provide a more personal experience, and the proprietors are frequently very informed about the various Champagnes they provide.

The Champagne Tasting Experience: When tasting Champagne, it's essential to pay attention to each glass's appearance, aroma, and flavor. Champagne's appearance can differ significantly based on the blend, and its aroma can be anything from fruity to yeasty to floral. Finally, based on the Champagne's style, the flavor may be sweet, dry, or somewhere in between.

Champagne is a versatile beverage that pairs well with a wide range of meals. The likes of cheese, seafood, and even popcorn are some common combinations. Food pairings are a common feature of the tasting experiences offered by Champagne houses and tasting areas.

Other Activities: Reims and Épernay offer a wide range of additional activities in addition to Champagne sampling.

These consist of touring the charming old towns, going to the magnificent Notre-Dame de Reims church, and flying in a hot air balloon over the vineyards.

Overall, visiting the Champagne region for a day trip from Paris is a wonderful opportunity to experience its splendor and cuisine. Just be sure to reserve your excursions and tastings in advance because they can get very busy during the busiest time of the year.

Normandy D-Day Beaches: A Historic and Scenic Tour

The D-Day beaches are among the most well-known landmarks in Normandy, one of France's historically important regions. For history buffs and anyone interested in learning more about this significant period in history, viewing the beaches and other places connected with the D-Day invasion is a must-do experience. This region played a significant role in the events that led up to the end of World War II.

Here is a list of some of the most significant locations to see and things to do while on a D-Day trip of Normandy:

One of the most well-known D-Day landing locations was Omaha Beach, where American troops encountered fierce German resistance. With a memorial and museum devoted to the events of June 6, 1944, the beach is now a serene place for contemplation and remembrance.

Utah Beach is home to a museum that explores the specifics of the operation and the experiences of the soldiers who took part. Utah Beach is another significant American landing location. The beach and its surroundings, which have been kept as they were during the conflict, are also open to visitors.

Visitors can still see the craters and other signs of the fierce combat that occurred at Pointe du Hoc, the dramatic cliffside site of a daring American assault on a German gun battery. The location also provides breathtaking views of the sea.

Sainte-Mère-Église: During the invasion, American soldiers parachuted into this charming Norman town, and one unfortunate paratrooper landed on the renowned church spire. Visitors can now explore the church and exhibition and discover more about the town's contribution to the conflict.

Over 9,000 American troops who lost their lives during the invasion of Normandy are buried at the somber Normandy American Cemetery and Memorial. With aisles of white crosses and stars of David set against a background of undulating hills and the sea, the cemetery is immaculately kept.

The Bayeux Tapestry, a masterpiece from the Middle Ages that portrays the events leading up to the Norman Conquest of England in 1066, is located in the picturesque town of Bayeux. For both art and history enthusiasts, the tapestry is a must-see, and the town itself is brimming with quaint boutiques, cafés, and buildings.

The Normandy region is renowned for its mouthwatering apples and the alcoholic beverages produced from them, such as Calvados (apple brandy) and cider. Visitors can take tours of nearby orchards and distilleries and taste these delectable delights.

The history of World War II is brought to life through a tour of the D-Day sites and surrounding regions in Normandy. This stunning and fascinating area of France has something to offer everyone, regardless of your interests in history, nature, or cuisine.

The Loire Valley: Castles, Wine, and More

The Loire Valley is a stunning area located just a few hours from Paris by train and is renowned for its magnificent châteaux, rolling hills, charming villages, and world-famous wines. The Loire Valley is home to some of France's most impressive architectural works, from opulent palaces to charming manor homes. The Loire Valley is a must-see when in France, whether you're interested in history, art, or just the good life.

The Loire Valley's past

The Loire Valley has a lengthy past that goes back to the Paleolithic era. Important conflicts from the Hundred Years' War and the Wars of Religion were once fought in this area. During the Renaissance, it was also a preferred getaway for French kings and nobles, who constructed many of the magnificent châteaux that still exist today.

Residences in the Loire Valley

More than 300 châteaux, each with a distinctive history and architectural design, can be found in the Loire Valley. The two most well-known châteaux are Château de Chenonceau, a stunning Renaissance palace constructed over the River Cher, and Château de Chambord, a grand palace with over 400 rooms and a unique double helix staircase.

Loire Valley wine tasting

The white wines made from the Sauvignon Blanc grape are especially well-known from the Loire Valley. Visitors can sample various wines, go on excursions of nearby vineyards and wineries, and learn how wine is made.

Walking and bicycling through the Loire Valley

A haven for outdoor enthusiasts, the Loire Valley has miles of paths for biking and hiking through the countryside. Rent a bike, and travel the Loire River while traveling through quaint towns and vineyards.

Investigating the Loire Valley's Towns and Villages

The Loire Valley is full of quaint locations to discover, from medieval towns to small fishing communities. Explore the troglodyte caves in the hamlet of Rochemenier, or go to the town of Amboise to see the Château d'Amboise, where Leonardo da Vinci is rumored to have resided.

In the Loire Valley, cuisine

The Loire Valley produces some of France's top cuisine, specializing in dishes made with seasonal, nearby products. Try some regional specialities like tarte Tatin, an upside-down apple tart, and rillettes, a type of pâté made with pork.

Events and Festivals in the Loire Valley

The renowned Fête des Vins in Tours and the International Garden Festival at Chaumont-sur-Loire are just two of the many festivals and events held throughout the year in the Loire Valley. In the Loire Valley, there is something for everyone, regardless of your interests in music, art, or cuisine.

The Loire Valley is a must-visit location for anyone visiting France because there is so much to see and do there.

Printed in Great Britain
by Amazon